YOUNG WATER PROTECTORS
A STORY ABOUT STANDING ROCK

COPYRIGHT 2018 © ASLAN AND KELLY TUDOR

ISBN: 978-1723305689

A **Water Protector** is someone who protects water from getting polluted. Companies are polluting the water by building things like oil pipelines under or near water ways.

Cannonball River, North Dakota

As Native Americans we want to protect the Earth and water from getting polluted and harmed because these are sacred lands and waters to us. We want to keep our homelands from getting harmed.

The Standing Rock Sioux Tribe is a Native nation of Dakota and Lakota peoples. Their reservation is located in North and South Dakota. Their lands use to be much bigger because of the **Treaty of Fort Laramie,** an agreement made a long time ago.

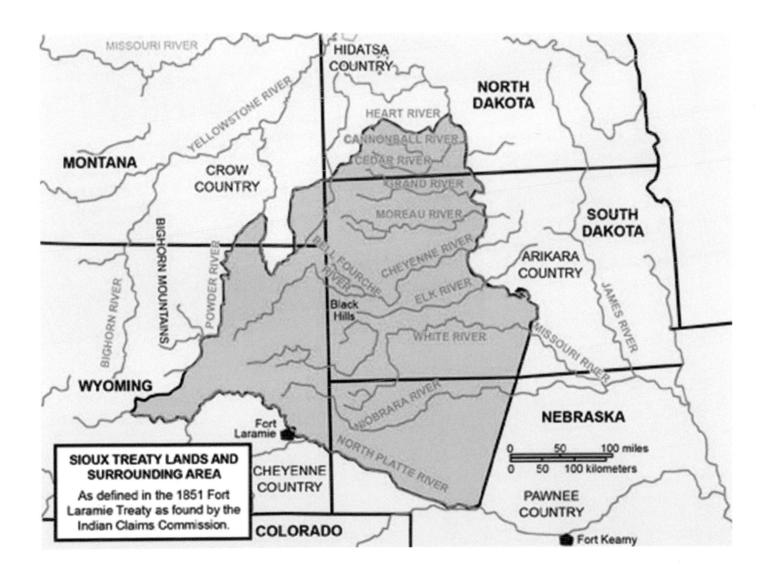

PEOPLE A LONG TIME AGO DID NOT RESPECT THAT AND TOOK THE LAND WITHOUT PERMISSION SO THAT THE RESERVATION BECAME MUCH SMALLER. THE LAND IS CALLED **UNCEDED TREATY TERRITORY** BECAUSE THE LAKOTA PEOPLE DID NOT GIVE UP THE LAND.

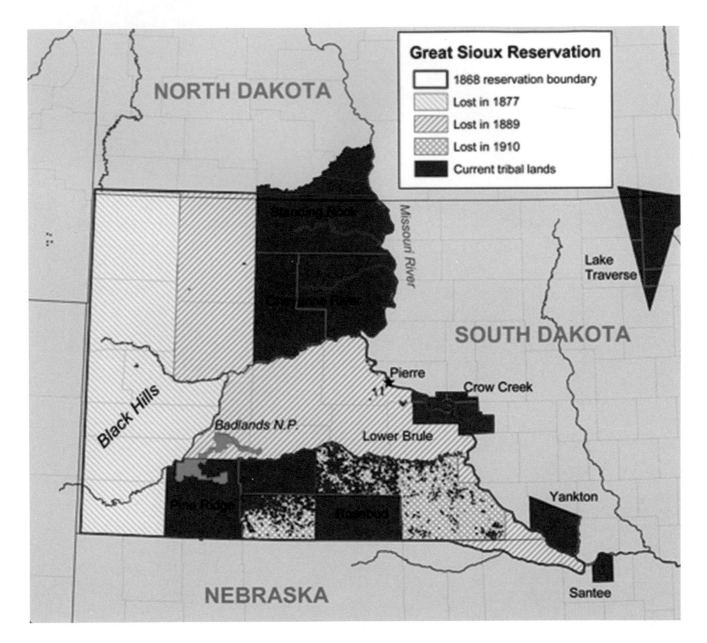

A COMPANY WAS TRYING TO BUILD AN OIL PIPELINE UNDER THE MISSOURI RIVER, WHICH IS STANDING ROCK'S DRINKING WATER SUPPLY. THE PIPELINE IS CALLED THE DAKOTA ACCESS PIPELINE. THE LAND AND WATER WHERE THE PIPELINE WAS BEING BUILT IS THEIR TREATY LAND.

WHEN PIPELINES ARE BUILT, THEY END UP LEAKING AND POLLUTING THE LAND AND WATER. IF THE DAKOTA ACCESS PIPELINE WERE TO LEAK, IT WOULD MAKE THE WATER FOR THE STANDING ROCK SIOUX TRIBE UNDRINKABLE.

IN LAKOTA, MNI WICONI MEANS "WATER IS LIFE."

Youth from Standing Rock started a Water Protector's camp to protect their water. It was called **Sacred Stone Camp**. They asked people to come and join them to help them protect their water. A lot of people came to help and a new camp started. It was called **Oceti Sakowin Camp**.

I went to North Dakota to the Oceti Sakowin camp in August 2016. I was 8 years old. I went with my mom, my little sister and some friends.

Every day we went to the gates where they were building the pipeline. The morning started with traditional Lakota prayers. Each day we were trying to stop them from building the pipeline.

The kids there helped protest and also played together. We sang traditional songs with everyone. People painted messages of resistance and posted flags from their Native nations.

Every day, warriors on horses rode through camp and led everyone on a march up to the pipeline construction site. They painted their horses and faces with traditional designs. One of them told me I have **WARRIOR HAIR**, because I keep it long.

In camp we slept in a tent. Others slept in tipis, busses and RVs. We ate food together and at night we had big fires and met Native Americans from all over. People sang round dance songs at night.

Camp started small and there were only other Native Americans there. Then camp grew rapidly. After we left, camp grew to around 10,000 people and it became one of the largest cities in North Dakota. They built a traditional Lakota school, several kitchens, a general store, a medical compound and many other things.

We came back in October 2016. Camp was huge when we got there. There were around 5000 people there. There were a lot of tipis and tents. It was much bigger than in August. There were Native people and non-Native people there this time.

I WENT TO THE TRADITIONAL LAKOTA SCHOOL THAT WAS IN CAMP. IT WAS CALLED THE DEFENDERS OF THE WATER SCHOOL. I LEARNED ABOUT A TYPE OF CORN MADE BY THE PUBELO PEOPLES. WE SANG LAKOTA SONGS. THEY HAD A LIBRARY IN THE SCHOOL. I READ BOOKS BY NATIVE AUTHORS. MY MOM WORKED IN THE MEDICAL TENT IN CAMP. SHE IS AN EMT.

We got to stay in a tipi with a friend. It was warm inside because there was a fire. It was pretty cold outside so it felt nice to sleep in the tipi.

The pipeline was still being built. People from camp went to different construction sites each day. It wasn't too safe for kids out there, so we stayed in camp.

Between August 2016 and February 2017, tens of thousands of people passed through this camp. People came from every continent of the world, including celebrities, politicians, and tribal representatives from over 500 Native nations. It was the largest Native gathering in history and the largest unity between different Native Nations we have ever had. The pipeline was delayed, but finished in summer of 2017. The Standing Rock Sioux Tribe is still fighting it in court.

Mni Wiconi
Water is Life

ABOUT THE AUTHOR

Thank you to the Standing Rock Sioux Tribe for the camp and the resistance to the pipeline. Thank you to my mom for helping me write this book. Thank you to everyone who helps fight pipelines and for Native rights.

Aslan Tudor is 10 years old.

He is a citizen of the **Lipan Apache Tribe** of Texas. He and his family live in Indianapolis, Indiana and are moving home to Texas soon. Aslan has traditional hair, which for boys is long. He is a grass dancer and drummer. He wants to be an actor to help represent Native people well in film. He acts in local stage plays currently.

PHOTO CREDITS

HTTPS://EN.WIKIPEDIA.ORG/W/INDEX.PHP?TITLE=FILE:CANNONBALL%2COND.JPG

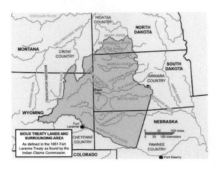

HTTPS://COMMONS.WIKIMEDIA.ORG/WIKI/FILE:SIOUX-TREATY-LANDS.PNG

HTTPS://COMMONS.WIKIMEDIA.ORG/WIKI/FILE:SIOUXRESERVATIONMAP.PNG

HTTP://BIT.LY/FLICKR-PHOTO

MORE FROM EAGLESPEAKER PUBLISHING

COLLECT 'EM ALL !!!

AUTHENTICALLY INDIGENOUS NAPI STORIES:
Napi and the Rock
Napi and the Bullberries
Napi and the Wolves
Napi and the Buffalo
Napi and the Chickadees
Napi and the Coyote
Napi and the Elk
Napi and the Gophers
Napi and the Mice
Napi and the Prairie Chickens
Napi and the Bobcat
... and many more Napi tales to come

AUTHENTICALLY INDIGENOUS GRAPHIC NOVELS:
UNeducation: A Residential School Graphic Novel
Napi the Trixster: A Blackfoot Graphic Novel
UNeducation, Vol 2

AUTHENTICALLY INDIGENOUS COLORING BOOKS:
Napi: A Coloring Experience
UNeducation: A Coloring Experience
Completely Capricious Coloring Collection
A Day at the Powwow (grayscale coloring)

AUTHENTICALLY INDIGENOUS KIDS BOOKS:
Teeias Goes to a Powwow (a series)

WWW.EAGLESPEAKER.COM